SHARING
YOUR FAITH

MADE EASY

D0829795

PUBLISHING

Sharing Your Faith Made Easy
Copyright © 2020 Rose Publishing, LLC

Published by Rose Publishing
An imprint of Hendrickson Publishing Group
Rose Publishing, LLC
P.O. Box 3473
Peabody, Massachusetts 01961-3473 USA
www.hendricksonpublishinggroup.com

The *Made Easy* series is a collection of concise, pocket-sized books that summarize key biblical teachings and provide clear, user-friendly explanations to common questions about the Christian faith. Find more *Made Easy* books at www.hendricksonrose.com.

All Scripture quotations, unless otherwise indicated, are taken from the Holy Bible, New International Version®, NIV®. Copyright ©1973, 1978, 1984, 2011 by Biblica, Inc.™ Used by permission of Zondervan. All rights reserved worldwide. www.zondervan.com The "NIV" and "New International Version" are trademarks registered in the United States Patent and Trademark Office by Biblica, Inc.™

Scripture quotations marked (NLT) are taken from the Holy Bible, New Living Translation, copyright © 1996, 2004, 2015 by Tyndale House Foundation. Used by permission of Tyndale House Publishers, Inc., Carol Stream, Illinois 60188. All rights reserved.

ISBN 9781628628258

Author: Len Woods

Gospel Illustrations: *24 Ways to Explain the Gospel* by Rose Publishing.

Printed in the United States of America
010720VP

CONTENTS

"But in your hearts revere Christ as Lord. Always be prepared to give an answer to everyone who asks you to give the reason for the hope that you have. But do this with gentleness and respect."

1 PETER 3:15–16

You've Been Commissioned by God!

Yes, *really*. Jesus has sent *all* his followers—not just pastors and missionaries—to share the good news of salvation (Matt. 28:18–20).

This is an exciting mission, but sometimes it can feel overwhelming. At times it might seem more like a scary burden than a joyous privilege. Maybe you've witnessed ugly confrontations between Christians and non-Christians over matters of faith. Perhaps you remember that one time you tried to talk about God with your friend and everything got really awkward. Maybe you're hesitant to even bring up anything religious with your family members, because every time you do, they just seem to get angry. No wonder the phrase "sharing your faith" sometimes makes us cringe.

The God who sent you on this mission of sharing the gospel message knows all this. He understands your fears and has not left you on your own. His Word has a lot to say to help you, encourage you, support you, and keep your mind and heart focused on what's most important.

In this book, we'll look at what God's Word says about sharing your faith. We'll tackle tough questions like these (and others):

- How can I talk about the Christian faith when I'm not a Bible scholar? What would I do if someone started firing hard questions at me?

- What exactly is the *gospel*, and how do I explain it to nonbelievers?

- Why would I, of all people, try to tell anyone about Jesus? Most days my life is a mess and my faith isn't exactly rock solid.

- Our culture is so polarized and secular—is it even possible to have civil, constructive spiritual discussions anymore?

- How can I begin talking about God with others? Where do I start?

For readers who want to wrestle with this subject further—or for those who want to read through this book with a few others (highly recommended!)—we've included some reflection and discussion questions at the end of this book.

SHARING YOUR FAITH: WHO? ME?!

It's one of the most remarkable scenes in world history.

A group of slack-jawed, wide-eyed folks on a mountainside, watching breathlessly as Jesus of Nazareth disappears straight up into the clouds.

Moments before, his last words to this small band of believers had been equal parts command and prophecy: "You will be my witnesses in Jerusalem, and in all Judea and Samaria, and to the ends of the earth" (Acts 1:8).

What?! Witnesses . . . *to the ends of the earth*?

Even more shocking is the group being commissioned.

A "dream team" of proven leaders? A "who's who" of religious scholars?

More like a "Who? *Them*?!" collection of nondescript nobodies.

These were Galilean fisherman and tax collectors, not the ancient equivalent of Harvard MBAs or seminary grads. Regular folks with plenty of flaws and almost as much doubt as faith. Individuals with shady backgrounds (in some cases) and quirky personalities, who often found it hard to get along.

And yet . . .

This was the group that would soon be empowered by God's Holy Spirit at Pentecost (Acts 2). *These* were the ones who would begin telling others about their life-changing experience with the crucified, resurrected Jesus.

This first generation of Christians had none of the resources we have, none of the technological blessings we enjoy. No publishing companies. No radio broadcasts. No cell networks or movie studios. They lacked cars and commercial jets, interstates and the internet. But each one had an authentic encounter with Jesus Christ and each one had a voice.

Saint Paul Preaching by Raphael

So they opened their mouths. They told their stories. And like ripples in a pond the gospel message began to spread in every direction. Even when hostile authorities cracked down, these simple followers of Jesus continued to speak up.

It wasn't long before the apostles and other Christian missionaries were fanning out across the Roman Empire (and beyond), leaving little groups of new believers in their wake. The good news of Jesus was spreading. The church of Jesus was growing.

And today? The upstart movement that began on a Jewish mountainside almost two millennia ago flourishes all over the world.

Fast forward to this moment. You are reading this sentence right now because countless people—regular folks who'd been changed by the gospel of Jesus—eagerly shared that good news with neighbors and strangers, who passed it on to their relatives and coworkers.

If they could do it, we can too. More than all the great material resources we have—smartphones and apps and Christian books—we have God's Word to guide us, his Spirit to strengthen us, and his people to encourage us.

And so the answer to the very common "Who? *Me*?!" question is, "Yes. *You*." You're a recipient of good news!

And good news, as we all know, is meant for sharing.

Qualities of an Effective Witness

Many Christians assume they need a seminary degree, or at least hours and hours of training, before they are "qualified" to talk to others about their faith. Not true. While formal evangelism training is always helpful (and highly recommended), it's not *necessary*. To point people to Jesus, what you need most is:

Grace—Jesus demonstrated a remarkable ability to meet people in their mess and to accept them and love them *as they were* (yet without condoning their lifestyles). Instead of fixating on their flaws, he saw what they could become (John 1:16).

Truth—A good witness (as our legal system daily reminds us) tells "the truth, the whole truth, and nothing but the truth." When the truth is hard, a good witness speaks it clearly, but always with gentleness and love (John 8:32).

Kindness—Nothing builds trust like demonstrating obvious concern and care for others. Being smart and articulate is fine, but being kind beats being clever every time (Colossians 3:12).

Humility—Nobody likes know-it-alls or people who are full of themselves. The most effective witnesses don't act superior; they mostly act stunned, shocked to be the recipients of God's love (Philippians 2:3).

Authenticity—If you've been bowled over by the fact that Jesus Christ would love you and give his life for you, if you are convinced he alone is the hope of the world, you have what it takes to shine as a witness. You'll be credible and compelling (2 Corinthians 5:11–21).

Even though the gospel has spread to much of the world—more than two billion people today claim some form of the Christian faith—the mission Jesus gave his followers is far from finished.

Think about your own situation. Unless you live on a desert island or in a remote cabin off the grid, you have people in your life—family members, friends, classmates, neighbors, and coworkers—who are far from God. Spiritually speaking, these people are all over the map: agnostics and Muslims, humanists and Hindus. They have faith in all sorts of things—science, astrology, Buddhism, or simply trying to be decent people. But they don't believe in Jesus.

> **You can learn to talk about your faith in a way that's life-giving, not relationship-killing.**

When you stop and remember this reality, your heart breaks. You don't want to bite your tongue. You want those around you to know the joy of a relationship with God, the peace that comes from staggering promises like John 3:16. What can you do? Can you learn to share your faith with others in a way that's constructive rather than destructive, winsome rather than weird? Is that even possible?

Absolutely. You're in the right book.

Discussing your Christian faith with unbelieving friends doesn't have to feel like walking a tightrope across the Grand Canyon without a safety net. It doesn't have to result in a nasty argument. You can learn to see the dreaded "E-word" (evangelism) in a new and positive light. More importantly, you can learn to talk about your faith in a way that's life-giving, not relationship-killing.

That's the purpose for this little book. Maybe we shouldn't overpromise. Maybe we can't exactly make sharing your faith *easy*; however, we can definitely make it a little *easier*.

By the time we're done, you'll . . .

- Be clearer on what the gospel is.

- Be motivated to pray and look for opportunities to talk about your faith.

- Know some simple, creative ways to start spiritual conversations.

- Have a better feel for what to say (and what not to say).

- Learn how you can tell your own spiritual story very naturally, briefly, in a way that's not pushy or preachy.

- Understand why it's so important to not only show the gospel with your life, but to tell it with your lips.

Maybe you're not yet convinced. Or maybe, if you're honest, you've got so much going on in your life right now that you don't spend much time thinking about the spiritual needs of others. If that's you, start with a prayer. Ask God for help.

A Prayer for Learning to Share Your Faith

Lord, give me a broken heart for people who don't know you. Help me to see people as you see them, to learn to love people with your perfect love.

Father, give me unbridled joy in my salvation. Remind me that I have good news—in fact, the best news ever.

God, give me opportunities to speak to others about you as I go about my day. Make me aware of holy moments, of divinely orchestrated encounters. And when those opportunities come, give me courage and boldness. Let me be filled with faith, not backed into a corner by fear.

Give me sensitivity to your leading, Holy Spirit. Keep me

from running ahead of you or being pushy with those who are not yet ready to respond to you. Make me an intriguing witness, not an irritating one. Set a guard, O Lord, over my mouth. When I speak, let me say only what you want said.

Give me power, Father. I am weak. My words are impotent. But you are God Almighty and nothing—no heart—is too hard for you to pierce.

Lord, give me a gracious, gentle spirit. Remind me that unbelievers (even the really angry ones) are not my enemy; they are captives of my enemy. May my attitudes, words, and deeds demonstrate the love, joy, peace, patience, and kindness of your Spirit.

Jesus, give me tenacity and a persevering heart. Your Word makes it clear that we are in a battle for souls. Sometimes the struggle is fierce and long and exhausting. Grant me the diligence and grit to keep at it, to dig in, and to keep reaching out.

Lord of life, lastly, give me the amazing blessing of seeing others come alive spiritually.

In your name I ask these things. Amen.

WHY ARE SPIRITUAL CONVERSATIONS SO HARD?

As we dig into the whys and hows of sharing our faith, it might be wise to first wrap our minds around some basic terminology:

A Short Lexicon of Salvation

Conversion—This word conveys the idea of turning away from one's old life of sin and turning to a new life of trusting and following Jesus (see Acts 15:3); it's related to the idea of *repentance*.

Evangelism—In the New Testament, the Greek word for gospel is *euangelion* (look familiar?) One who proclaims the gospel is called an *evangelist* (2 Timothy 4:5). And when evangelists declare or tell the good news of Jesus' life, death, and resurrection, they are said to be *evangelizing* or doing *evangelism* (Acts 14:7).

Faith—As a noun ("I shared my faith with a friend"), *faith* refers to the essential beliefs of Christians. Used in a verbal sense ("I put my faith in Jesus"), it refers to believing in, trusting in, or placing confidence in Christ.

Gospel—The word *gospel* literally means "good news" or "glad tidings." In the Bible it refers to the story and message of Jesus, the Son of God, who came—in his own words—"to seek and save the lost." (We'll talk in greater detail about this shortly.)

Justification—This is God's declaration that sinful people are "not guilty" when they place their faith in Jesus (see Romans 5:1).

Lost—The New Testament word *lost* means "to be perishing or ruined." It's used in the gospels, but it's not found in the rest of the New Testament.

Proselytizing—This English word, which comes straight from the Greek language (Acts 2:11), has negative cultural connotations. However, it really just refers to helping an interested person become a *proselyte* (a convert or adherent) of a religion. Before and during the time of Christ, some non-Jews willingly underwent a series of steps to become proselytes of the Jewish religion.

Reconciliation—This is the stunning idea that through believing the gospel, rebellious human creatures are brought back into a right relationship with the God they've defied (see Romans 5:10; Colossians 1:21–22).

Regeneration—This word means "to come alive from the dead" and refers to the gracious work of God in awakening the hearts and opening the eyes of sinners, of God making unbelievers hungry for and responsive to the gospel (Ephesians 2:5).

Repentance—The New Testament word (Luke 5:32) refers to "changing one's mind." The Old Testament idea means "to turn around." Putting those ideas together, repentance is seeing things in a new way and turning to a new way as a result. Some see repentance and faith as two sides of the same coin; others see them as synonymous.

Saved—The word *saved* simply means "rescued." Biblically, it can refer to deliverance from physical danger or to rescue from spiritual doom. To be saved in the ultimate spiritual sense (Mark 10:26–27) means to be forgiven by God and reconciled to him.

Witnessing—In our culture, a witness is someone who tells what they have seen, heard, or experienced. The Greek word *martys*, translated *witness*, is where we get our English word *martyr*. Strictly speaking, we are witnesses of Christ when we talk about our experience with him (Acts 1:8).

Now that we have a better grasp on the vocabulary often used to describe the good news of Jesus and the act of sharing it, let's examine why sharing your faith is such a challenge.

In truth, there are multiple reasons so many Christians shy away from engaging in evangelism.

Historical. Some people remember bad prior experiences and feel embarrassed. ("I did that once. What a disaster!")

Personal. Many believers feel personally inadequate or unqualified. ("I'm not trained to do that" or "I'm no Bible scholar!" or "My own spiritual life is pretty messy.")

Cultural. As society becomes more secular, it's easy to get skittish. ("What if I get labeled as a *bigoted Bible thumper*?" or "What if I alienate the very people I want to reach?" or "What if I catch heat from my boss?")

Spiritual. The Bible speaks of other powerful forces at work, and most Christians have experienced this phenomenon. ("Every time I think *I'm going to talk to my sister about spiritual matters tonight*, it's like something always pops up! It never seems to work out.")

Maybe you can relate?

Can God Use Imperfect Christians?

You bet! He can, and he *does*. In fact, broken souls (that are in the process of being healed and restored) are all the Lord has to work with (Romans 3:23)! This is one of the most astonishing takeaways from the Bible—God does his best work through flawed people! When you start thinking, "I'm disqualified from sharing my faith," remember these four truths:

We're all "under construction." Till the day we die, God will be working to make us like Jesus (Philippians 2:12–13). If you wait until you've "got it all together" to share your faith, you never will.

Everybody is hypocritical. Christians and non-Christians alike fail to live perfectly by whatever standards they set for themselves and others.

The issue isn't perfection (we won't reach that state until heaven); the issue is progress. Are you seriously following after Christ (even if that includes a lot of bumbling and stumbling)?

Humility and authenticity are huge. When unbelievers see believers blow it—then own their failures and do everything they possibly can to make things right—it's actually more powerful than if we'd never messed up.

Why Does Sharing Our Faith Feel Like Such a Fierce Battle?

Because it is a battle. According to the New Testament, evangelism is nothing less than spiritual warfare. Without trying to sound dramatic, sharing our faith is an effort to storm "the gates of hell" (Matthew 16:18). The holy mission Jesus calls us to? Using the gospel to liberate those held hostage by the devil.

We have a bitter enemy. The Holy Scriptures speak matter-of-factly about a real being known as the devil or Satan. In the New Testament, the apostle Paul calls him "the god of this age" and notes how he blinds "the minds of unbelievers, so that they cannot see the light of the gospel" (2 Corinthians 4:4). This means that when we even think about sharing our faith, the devil marshals "the spiritual forces of evil in the heavenly realms" (Ephesians 6:12) to oppose our efforts.

Satan is deadly. He's "a murderer" (John 8:44), Jesus said, a kind of spiritual terrorist. His only purpose is to cause (eternal) death, despair, and destruction. The last thing the devil wants is Spirit-filled believers joyfully telling unbelievers how to find the life that satisfies, the life that never ends. No wonder he works endlessly and diabolically to keep believers silent and to keep God's truth from taking root in people's hearts (Mark 4:1–20).

The devil will stop at nothing.

- He'll *lie* to you. ("Nobody is interested in hearing that stuff!")

- He'll *distract* you. ("Have that conversation another time. Right now you really need to _____.")

- He'll *accuse* you. ("Where do you get off thinking *you* have any business talking to others about Jesus? You're the *worst sinner ever*!")

- If none of those tactics work, he'll *threaten* you. ("Keep that up and you're not going to have a single friend left.")

- Or he'll *discourage* you. ("You know, you're not very effective at this. Why do you keep trying?")

- And if all these ploys fail, he'll try to *entice* you to give in to some sort of sinful temptation. He'd love to make you one more casualty in the great battle between good and evil.

For all these reasons the apostle Paul tells believers to be strong in the Lord and to put on the spiritual armor God has provided for us:

"Finally, be strong in the Lord and in his mighty power.
Put on the full armor of God, so that you can take
your stand against the devil's schemes.
For our struggle is not against flesh and blood,
but against the rulers, against the authorities,
against the powers of this dark world and against the
spiritual forces of evil in the heavenly realms.
Therefore put on the full armor of God, so that when
the day of evil comes, you may be able to stand your ground,
and after you have done everything, to stand.
Stand firm then, with the belt of truth buckled around
your waist, with the breastplate of righteousness in place,
and with your feet fitted with the readiness that
comes from the gospel of peace.
In addition to all this, take up the shield of faith, with which
you can extinguish all the flaming arrows of the evil one.
Take the helmet of salvation and the sword
of the Spirit, which is the word of God.

And pray in the Spirit on all occasions
with all kinds of prayers and requests.
With this in mind, be alert and always keep on
praying for all the Lord's people.
Pray also for me, that whenever I speak, words may be given
me so that I will fearlessly make known the mystery of the
gospel, for which I am an ambassador in chains.
Pray that I may declare it fearlessly, as I should. "

—EPHESIANS 6:10–20

Ask God to help you get good at putting on (and taking up) all his divine resources. That way, when you engage in sharing your faith, you won't be unequipped and unprotected.

All these external, internal, and infernal factors aside, there is still this: The word *gospel* means "good news." Usually, people *love* good news. So why, when we share the good news about new life, don't people embrace it eagerly? Why isn't everyone clapping and cheering when we share our faith?

Why Do People Respond to the Gospel So Slowly?

People have used various metaphors to describe "coming to faith" and "maturing in faith." Some refer to the spiritual life as a *journey* (probably because the Bible talks so much about "walking with God" and "following Christ").

The New Testament also uses *agricultural* imagery to show that spiritual birth and growth is a process. It pictures God's truth being planted, like a seed, in a person's heart. This can happen via a sermon, through reading the Bible, or as a result of a lunchroom conversation about Jesus. Over time, God sends other believers along to water that seed (1 Corinthians 3:6). Eventually—maybe in a few weeks or months, or perhaps over many years—the seed germinates, grows, and bears fruit. In the language of the book of Acts, God "opens [a person's] heart to respond" (Acts 16:14). They believe the good news about Jesus! There is a spiritual harvest at last! The result is a changed life on earth—and a joyous celebration in heaven (Luke 15:7).

To help believers grasp this idea that spiritual life and growth is a process or journey (and to illustrate the truth that people are at very different places), various writers—James Engel in the mid-1970s was one of the first—have used number lines (often going from -10 to 0 to +10) to illustrate how people come to Jesus, find salvation, and undergo spiritual growth. These assorted scales and charts (you can find them all over the internet) attempt to describe common steps people take or stages they pass through in their journey to faith and maturity in Christ.

Here's one example:

+6 The maturing Christian leader who is shepherding and discipling others

+4 The committed disciple who is learning, growing, and serving

+2 The new believer who is taking baby steps in the faith

0 The individual who puts their faith in Jesus (this is salvation, or conversion, or the new birth)

-2 The person who is almost convinced that Jesus is who he claims to be

-4 The "seeker" (religious or not) who becomes intrigued by Jesus' life and teachings and starts asking a lot of questions

-6 The open-minded skeptic who is willing to explore various belief systems; or

The religious but disenchanted non-Christian who is unsure about their faith and "looking around"

-8 The quiet agnostic who has zero interest in spiritual matters; or

The fiercely devoted follower of a non-Christian religion or belief system

-10 The atheist who has strong negative feelings about God, the Bible, and religion

Do you see the progression? This is what coming to faith looks like for many.

Don't get hung up on the numbers or the corresponding descriptions. Scales like this certainly aren't "inspired"; they are only for illustrative purposes. Their point is simply to show that "sharing our faith" can look very different, depending on where the people around us are in life.

Let's say you have a colleague who's angry at God. One day she is bitterly blaming God for her mother's death. The next day she's insisting that God doesn't exist! Perhaps if you are a faithful friend and a Christlike example to her, the Lord will use you over time to help her move from -9 on the scale to -6. She's not yet a believer, but God is clearly at work. Maybe when she moves in three years, a Christian in her new city will help her get to -2 . . . and then lead her to faith!

The great thing about charts like this is that they remind us that "sharing our faith" isn't just when we hand a gospel tract to someone and they decide on the spot to put their faith in Jesus. To be sure, when that happens, it's a remarkable experience. There's nothing like it! But it also makes God smile if you sit and have a good spiritual conversation with your Muslim friend—even if she says she isn't (yet) eager to read through the gospel of Mark with you.

A few pages back we suggested a prayer for your own heart. How about these prayers for the people you'd like to reach?

10 Prayers for the Unbelievers in Your Life

(Insert the names of unbelievers you know in the blanks below.)

1. That _____ might develop a curiosity about God and a hunger to understand God's Word (Acts 8:26–35).

2. For _____ to seek God, to "reach out for him and find him" (Acts 17:27).

3. For God to use me (or someone else) to "open _____ eyes and turn them from darkness to life and from the power of Satan to God" (Acts 26:18).

4. For God to pour out his grace on _____ (Acts 15:11).

5. For God to "grant _____ repentance leading them to a knowledge of the truth" (2 Timothy 2:25).

6. For God to soften the heart of _____ (Ephesians 4:18).

7. For the Lord to open _____ heart to respond to the gospel (Acts 16:14).

8. For God to "make _____ alive with Christ" (Ephesians 2:5).

9. For _____ to "believe in the Lord Jesus and . . . be saved" (Acts 16:31).

10. For God to make _____ a "new creation" (2 Corinthians 5:17).

WHAT EXACTLY AM I SUPPOSED TO SAY?

In our lexicon of "salvation" words a few pages back, we mentioned the *gospel*. That good news message is what we deliver when we share our faith. So what exactly does God's good news entail?

What Is the Gospel?

As we've mentioned, the word *gospel*, found just over a hundred times in the New Testament, comes from the Greek word *euangelion*. (Again, that explains where we get our English words *evangelism*, *evangelist*, and *evangelize*.) *Gospel* means "good news." It's not strictly a religious word. In ancient times, kings often sent heralds throughout their kingdoms to proclaim various kinds of "gospels," like a royal birth or a great military victory.

The New Testament uses the word *gospel* in connection with the coming of Jesus. His life, death, and resurrection are presented as the ultimate good news. Why? Because Jesus declared himself the Messiah (John 4:25–26), the ultimate Savior/King promised by God, who came:

- "to seek and to save the lost" (Luke 19:10) by "giv[ing] his life as a ransom" (Matthew 20:28);

- to abolish death (2 Timothy 1:10); and

- to offer eternal life as a free gift to those who trust in him (John 3:16).

In one of his New Testament letters, the apostle Paul, a towering figure in the early church, summarized the gospel of Jesus this way:

> Now, brothers and sisters, I want to remind you of the gospel I preached to you, which you received and on which you have taken your stand . . . that Christ died for our sins according to the Scriptures, that he was buried, that he was raised on the third day according to the Scriptures. (1 Corinthians 15:1, 3–4)

That's it, in one short paragraph. That is the good news, the *great* news, the *fantastic* news that Paul preached (and that believers have been sharing for almost two thousand years. In just a few words we see a stunning announcement about our condition, God's provision, and the decision we need to make.

Our Condition

Notice Paul mentions Christ dying "for our *sins*." (There's a word that gets thrown around a lot in spiritual conversations.) What exactly does *sin* mean?

We typically think of sin as the regrettable things we do or the awful things we say. Actually, sin goes much deeper than that. External actions like lying, flying off the handle, looking at pornography, being cruel toward others . . . these are mere *outer* symptoms of a much deeper, *inner* problem. Before sin is ever an action, it's a condition.

In the divine story the Bible tells, we see Earth's first couple essentially declaring their independence from God (you can read about this in Genesis 3). *That* is sin in its essence: turning away from God, the source of life, and trying to find life and meaning apart from him.

The ancient Scriptures say that as the descendants of Adam and Eve, we've inherited their same wayward nature. Rebellion is in our spiritual DNA. In fact, the natural, default, 24/7 setting of every human heart is the tendency to tell God to take a hike when he tells us how to live. We resent his rules and rage against his commands.

And the consequence of our turning away from God? Awful. Devastating. Catastrophic. The apostle Paul described the human race as being in a grim state of spiritual death (Romans 6:23). We are separated from the giver of life. We are "God's enemies" (Romans 5:10).

If you're thinking, *That doesn't sound like good news* . . . you're right, of course! Fortunately, in the passage cited above, Paul explains what God did about our problem.

God's Provision

Notice that Paul declares that "Christ died for our sins . . . he was buried . . . he was raised." In other words, it is the death of Jesus "for our sins" and Christ's resurrection to life that opens the door for sinners to experience the divine blessings of forgiveness and new, eternal life. The good news that Paul and the other apostles announced is that when the human race was (justifiably) on a kind of spiritual death row because of sin, Jesus came and acted as our substitute (Romans 5:8). He willingly took the punishment we deserved. Thus, in Christ's death on the cross, we see two realities:

- God's justifiable wrath against sin (he hates whatever ruins his creation) and

- God's remarkable love for sinners (he refuses to let us go).

By raising Jesus from the dead, God made it clear that his sacrifice for sin was acceptable. Now, as a risen Savior, Jesus *lives* to offer forgiveness and eternal life to any and all who turn to him.

Our Decision

Notice that Paul's comments in this ancient letter are directed to people who "received" this good news.

To receive the gospel is to embrace it. In the New Testament, *receive* is sometimes a synonym for *believe* (John 1:12). In other words, we put our trust in the message of the gospel. We believe in the One the message is about. Or, in Paul's other words, we take our stand on it. We make it the foundation of our lives.

Salvation isn't something we work for. It's a free gift!

Do you see? The gospel isn't a marketing campaign to get people to come to church. It's not a lecture about cleaning up your life, or a list of rules we follow in order to work our way back into God's favor. The gospel is the shocking announcement that God has come *to* us and *for* us in Jesus! The New Testament is explicit: Salvation isn't something we work for. We can't earn it. It's a free gift (John 4:10; Romans 6:23; Ephesians 2:8–9)! There's nothing for us to do, because Jesus has already done everything necessary.

The only questions are: Will we trust in Jesus? Will we believe in the gospel? Will we take our stand on the historical truth of Christ's life, death, and resurrection and receive him? We have a big decision to make.

We can explain the good news of Jesus using lots of other Bible passages, but 1 Corinthians 15:1, 3–4 is one of the most succinct. It shows the message and meaning of the gospel in one short paragraph.

Why So Angry?

When Paul spoke about his experience on the Damascus Road, his listeners responded by saying, "Rid the earth of him! He's not fit to live!" (Acts 22:22). While that response was extreme, it reflects a broader pattern of people responding to the gospel with anger. Why do some people get so furious at God's good news? What's upsetting about a gracious, no-strings-attached offer of forgiveness and eternal life?

Simply this: The gospel, before it's good news, is offensive news. The gospel says that people are flawed and rebellious and lost. To human pride, this announcement is like a punch in the throat. Though the gospel is a message of rescue, inherent in that message is the idea that you *need* rescue. For someone who is hearing the gospel for the first time, the idea that they're guilty of sin might come as quite a shock—not to mention the fact that someone died in order to save them. Sinful people recoil at this truth—until God takes off the blinders. Don't be too surprised if people get angry when you share your faith: they may need time and space to come to terms with these new ideas.

Understanding God's Grace

One of the things to keep in mind while you're preparing to share your faith is that many people, including some Christians, struggle to internalize the good news of God's grace. Even people who have heard the gospel many times can get stuck in a mind-set where they're focused on earning grace, instead of accepting it as a free gift. This misunderstanding of grace puts the emphasis on human behavior, or trying to be acceptable to God by being moral or nice or helpful. Instead of trusting God, they count on their own perceived goodness to win God's approval, relying on their own efforts to qualify them for grace and eternal life. They focus on trying their best, which is shorthand for "I believe my salvation is dependent on how I live." And that belief is the opposite of the gospel.

> We can only *accept* God's free gift of eternal life; we can never *earn* it.

Instead, we want to communicate (and remember ourselves!) that salvation is a gift to the undeserving, not a reward to the deserving (Romans 3:20–30; Ephesians 2:8–9; 2 Timothy 1:9; Titus 3:4–5). We can only *accept* God's free gift of eternal life; we can never *earn* it. People are made right with God not by what they do, but solely by what Jesus did.

After reading this, you may be thinking two things:

1

"I'm not sure I've ever put my trust in Christ alone."

If that's the case, you can put your faith in Jesus right now, right where you are. It's not complicated. There aren't any hoops to jump through. Simply express to God your desire to be forgiven, to be right with him. There's no "right" way to say that. Just tell the Lord you are saying, "Yes!" to all that he has done for you. Embrace him. Tell Jesus you are, by faith, accepting his free gift of salvation. Or, to borrow a phrase from another of Paul's ancient letters, ask Christ to "make his home" in your heart as you trust in him (Ephesians 3:17 NLT).

2

"I know the idea of sharing good news should excite me, but if I'm honest, I just feel kind of blah."

Because we are on a journey to maturity and we're works in progress (that is, "working out" our salvation even as God "works in" us—see Philippians 2:12–13), we don't experience nonstop spiritual ecstasy. Living in a fallen world with minds that aren't yet fully renewed (Romans 12:2), our faith in Christ tends to swell and shrink, and our passion for Christ tends to come and go.

This means there will be days when, if we're honest, the good news of Jesus doesn't exactly give us goose bumps. We hear rich words like "grace" or "salvation" and we . . . yawn. What then? How do we recapture a holy enthusiasm for the gospel?

How about spending a few minutes meditating on all that happened to you when the Lord saved you?

The Difference Jesus Makes

BEFORE BELIEVING THE GOSPEL I WAS . . .	SINCE BELIEVING THE GOSPEL I AM . . .
Spiritually dead (Romans 5:12; Ephesians 2:1, 5)	**Spiritually alive** (John 3; 5:24–26; Ephesians 2:5)
Lost (Isaiah 53:6; Mark 6:34)	**Found** (Matthew 18:12; Luke 15)
Spiritually blind (John 9:39–41; 2 Corinthians 4:4)	**Able to see spiritual realities** (Luke 4:18–19; 24:31; John 9:39)
In darkness (Matthew 4:16; John 3:19; Acts 26:18; Romans 13:12; Eph. 5:8)	**In the light** (John 8:12; Ephesians 5:8; Colossians 1:13)
Ignorant of God (Acts 3:17; 17:23; Ephesians 4:18; 1 Timothy 1:13)	**Coming to know God in wisdom** (Luke 1:77; 1 Corinthians 2:12; Ephesians 1:8, 17)
At war with God (his enemy) (Romans 5:10; Colossians 1:21)	**At peace with God (his friend)** (John 15:14–15; Romans 5:1)
A child of wrath (Ephesians 2:3)	**A child of God** (John 1:12; Romans 8:15; Galatians 4:6; 1 John 3:2)

BEFORE BELIEVING THE GOSPEL I WAS . . .	SINCE BELIEVING THE GOSPEL I AM . . .
Under God's just condemnation (Romans 1:18; 2:5; 5:18)	**Justified and pardoned by God** (Romans 5:18)
Indebted to God (Colossians 2:14; 1 Peter 1:19	**Ransomed and redeemed** (Matthew 20:28; 1 Corinthians 6:20; 7:23; Hebrews 9:15)
Enslaved to sin and in bondage (John 8:34; Romans 6:6, 16, 20, 22)	**Free** (John 8:36; Romans 6:17–18, 22; Galatians 5:1, 13)
Dirty and impure (Romans 6:19; 1 Thessalonians 4:7)	**Clean and pure** (Hebrews 9:14; 1 John 1:9)

These things are true even when we don't *feel* them.

An old pastor used to tell his people, "You need to preach the gospel to yourself every day." That's wise counsel. As you do that, ask God to "restore . . . the joy of your salvation" (Psalm 51:12).

The fact is, when your heart is overflowing with gratitude over all God has done to save you, you'll be a more engaging, attractive witness. People are drawn to those who are authentically passionate.

We're the recipients of really, really good news. And we have the privilege of sharing that message with others.

Let's look now at how to do that in an effective way.

HOW CAN I SHARE MY FAITH EFFECTIVELY?

Okay, you've got a good sense of what the gospel message is: it's an announcement about our condition, God's provision, and the decision we need to make to trust in Jesus. Before you start spreading the news, it's helpful to stop and recall a few realities:

Five Things to Remember about the People You Know

1 Everybody Is Looking for Meaning

God made us humans to be happy . . . happy *in him*!

But Adam and Eve, thinking they could find a greater happiness than what God offered, turned away from the One who is perfect Love and ultimate Good. That's the shocking story of the human race.

Spiritually speaking, we all have Adam and Eve's rebellious tendencies in us. And so it is that every person born into this world heads off on a restless search for meaning as soon as they can crawl. We are all looking for something—anything—to satisfy the deep ache and emptiness within. Everywhere we look (including the mirror) we see men, women, boys, and girls who are wrapping their hearts around whatever they think will complete them, save them, and satisfy the deep longings of their heart. The great theologian and philosopher Augustine said it best some 1,600 years ago, "You have made us for yourself, O God, and our hearts are restless until they rest in you."

Every Person Has a Complicated Story

We all have big things swirling in our lives and hearts—all the time. Each of us is a knotted mess of dreams and desires, hurts and regrets, flaws and strengths. This is why depending on the day (or time of day) we might be upbeat and hopeful, or grumpy and discouraged. And it's why we need to remember that great line that's been attributed to everyone from Plato to Philo to Ian Maclaren, "Be kind. For everyone you meet is fighting a hard battle." That cynical coworker, that mean neighbor, that surly kid in your class—chances are, if you knew what their lives are *really* like, their behavior would make a lot more sense.

Sharing the gospel isn't lecturing people about the poor choices they've made. It's not telling them to clean up their lives. It's saying, "Here is the One your heart was made for. And this is the story you were made to live in."

Some People Have Legitimate Problems with Christianity

You likely have neighbors, coworkers, classmates, and roommates who grew up in Christian homes where they saw a not-so-healthy version of the Christian faith. Perhaps they attended a dysfunctional church that operated by guilt rather than grace, legalism instead of love.

It's sad but true. Though church should be the one place where wounded people experience healing, too many times it's a place where broken people find even more pain! Be sensitive to such folks. They're hurt, angry, and disillusioned. Listen to their stories. Weep with the ones who weep. Express your sorrow that they encountered such things. Then ask God to use you to help these wounded souls see a more accurate picture of the Christian faith.

> **Sharing the gospel is saying, "Here is the One your heart was made for. And this is the story you were made to live in."**

Others Are Watching You Closely

If you claim to be a follower of Jesus, people will watch to see if what you say matches up with how you live. As the old saying goes, you are the only "Bible" some people are reading. This doesn't mean you have to be perfect—in fact, you'll never get there in this life. It does mean that when you mess up in front of the very people you are trying to reach, own it. Be humble. Admit your flaws. Ask forgiveness. The fact that you blow it is less important than what you do afterward.

You Catch More Flies with Honey Than with Vinegar

If people are going to walk away "offended," let it be because they are wrestling with the sobering claims of Jesus, not because they are fuming over the harsh or insensitive way you talked to them.

So how does it happen? How can we get folks talking about life's biggest questions without it feeling forced, or like we are being pushy spiritual salespeople? How about some simple, honest questions?

Spiritual Conversation Starters

- I notice you're wearing a cross. For you, is that more of a faith statement or a fashion statement?

- What kind of religious background, if any, do you have? What was that experience like for you growing up?

- I just read a book about faith [this one]. It got me thinking about religion, God, church, Jesus. What do you think about all that?

- I was reading a book the other day [this one] that mentioned how hard it is for people to have spiritual conversations. Why do you think our culture is so leery of those topics?

- Do you believe in the supernatural? Ghosts? Spirits? The devil? God?

- What do you think happens to us after we die? Do you believe in some kind of afterlife?

- What would you say is the purpose of life?

- (When a friend or neighbor says something negative about faith or Christians or the Bible . . .) That's interesting. I'd love to hear more about why you feel that way.

- (When religious holidays approach . . .) How do you celebrate on Easter (or Christmas or Lent or Ramadan, etc.)?

- (When Christians are in the news . . .) What do you think about that? What do you suppose Jesus would say about that?

- (When "God" comes up in conversation with a coworker . . .) Just out of curiosity, what do you think about the whole idea of God? Do you think there really is a Creator? If so, what do you think God is like?

- If God really exists, would you want to know God?

- What do you think of Jesus? Do you think he is who he claimed to be?

If you sense a person is comfortable (or even eager) talking about spiritual matters, sometimes before you pull out a Bible or start quoting verses, you can talk briefly about your experience with Christ. It's easier than you think.

Sharing Your Story

If I told you to spend fifteen minutes at lunch tomorrow telling a coworker or classmate all about the Battle of the Bulge and why it matters, how would you feel? I'm guessing that unless you're a military scholar or a World War II history buff, you'd feel inadequate and in over your head.

But suppose I said, "Tell your lunch companion tomorrow the story of how you met your best friend and what they mean to you." You wouldn't struggle for a second. You wouldn't wonder what to say, or worry about getting your facts wrong. Why? *Because it's a story from your personal experience.* You were there. It happened to you. (If anything, you'd find it difficult to limit your story to only fifteen minutes!)

This is the reason sharing your own faith story is so powerful. A testimony—as some Christians call it—is a brief spiritual autobiography. It's your own unique, firsthand account of how you met Christ—and the difference he's made in your life.

People can argue over spiritual concepts—what "faith" means or what the death of Jesus accomplished. They can debate controversial passages in the Bible. But no one can deny your story. The fact that Jesus freed you from shame or addiction or bitterness against the person who betrayed you is not up for discussion. No one can legitimately say, "That didn't happen" or "That's not true."

And here's another benefit of learning to talk about your spiritual experience. It's not like you're launching into a long, religious lecture. Let's face it, most folks would rather hear a story than a sermon any day. So get good at telling your faith story.

How to Tell Your Story

If you want some great examples of how to share your testimony, read the book of Acts, paying close attention to the apostle Paul. After telling the story of how Paul met the resurrected Jesus on the Damascus Road (Acts 9:1–19), Luke (the writer of Acts) records Paul sharing his "spiritual bio" on two separate occasions with two different groups of people (Acts 21:37–22:22 and Acts 26:1–29).

In each instance Paul talked about:

1. his life before meeting Jesus;

2. the details surrounding his conversion; and

3. how his life began to change after becoming a follower of Christ.

This simple format can help us as we tell our salvation story to others. Consider a few examples:

BEFORE I CAME TO FAITH	"I grew up in a Christian home, going to church *all the time*. I didn't always see the point of it, and sometimes I dreamed of being able to skip church every once in a while."
WHEN I CAME TO FAITH	"When I was in college, I did skip church—a lot. It felt liberating at first, but after a while I realized that something was missing. I got involved in a campus ministry, and one night, I knelt down beside my bed and asked Jesus to be Lord of my life."
SINCE I CAME TO FAITH	"I've been learning what it means to follow Jesus. And while my life isn't perfect, he is slowly changing my desires. More and more, I just want to love God and love people."
BEFORE I CAME TO FAITH	"I was the most religious person you'd ever meet, but the truth is that I was *still* miserable and empty inside."
WHEN I CAME TO FAITH	"One day I was reading in the Gospel of Matthew and it hit me: *I'm just like the Pharisees! Constantly judging people and thinking I'm better—when really, it's like I'm dead inside!* I was so aware that I was as far from God as anybody anywhere! I got on my knees and asked Jesus to forgive me and change me."
SINCE I CAME TO FAITH	"I'm coming to understand God's grace more and more. I used to be so harsh and judgmental toward irreligious people. Now God has given me a deep compassion for those who don't know him. I just want everyone to know Jesus."

BEFORE I CAME TO FAITH	"I came from a chaotic home—abuse, divorce. It was a mess. In high school I went off the rails: drinking heavily to numb the pain, sleeping around, trying to find love."
WHEN I CAME TO FAITH	"In college I had a Christian roommate who showed me and told me about the unconditional love of Jesus. I had a hard time believing he could love someone with my wild past. But when I hit rock bottom, I asked Christ to save me from anger and my promiscuous lifestyle, and he did! He took away those old desires that were killing me."
SINCE I CAME TO FAITH	"I've seen God replace my pain with his peace. I've learned to forgive my parents and now see myself the way God sees me—as a new person, a beloved child of God."

Do this exercise: Get out some paper (or create a new file in your computer) and take a few minutes to write your own testimony. Scribble (or type) a couple sentences or short paragraphs about your life before you put your faith in Jesus. Were you selfish, fearful, full of shame, or always angry? Did you struggle with insecurity or have a controlling personality? Talk about the specific problems that made you restless and that caused you to realize "My life isn't working" and "I need help." (NOTE: You don't have to go into gory details—just tell enough to let someone know you were not in a good place.) If you were raised Christian, write a few sentences about what it was like to grow up with Christian parents and go to church as a child.

Next write a brief summary of the circumstances that led to you placing your trust in Jesus. Did a parent or youth worker or coworker tell you about Christ? Was it a website or retreat that proved to be instrumental in helping you understand and believe the gospel? If you grew up in a Christian home, was there a specific moment when you decided to continue believing in Jesus as an adult? Again, you don't have to go on and on, just a few sentences:

> I went to a summer camp and heard a speaker explain that religion focuses on all the things we think *we have to do* to try to satisfy God . . . but the problem is that every religion has a different list! And there's also this: How can we ever know if we've done enough? Christianity is different. It focuses on *all that Jesus did* to satisfy God. He gave his life to pay for our sins and he rose from the dead. He did everything necessary. All we have to do is put our trust in him, in what he did for us. The speaker showed us that the Bible explains that salvation isn't a *reward* we try to earn. It's a gift we receive. That day at camp, I told God, "I am trusting Jesus. I accept your *gift* of forgiveness and salvation." Some days I'll admit: I don't *feel* saved or *feel* close to God. But I know that being right with God isn't based on how I feel. It's based on what Jesus did.

SHARE YOUR STORY

Or something like:

> I was visiting my sister. She had always been, well, sort of negative and gloomy; but on this particular visit she was upbeat and lighthearted. I'm telling you, the before and after difference was startling! I asked her, "What's going on? You're so . . . joyful. When did you become an optimist?" She laughed and proceeded to tell me about reading some book and giving her life to Christ. I was skeptical, rolling my eyes and shaking my head, but when I left her house she handed me the book. It's called *More Than a Carpenter*. When I got home, I read it. And then I couldn't stop thinking about it, so I reread it! I wrestled internally for a while, until I finally admitted: *I think what that book is saying about Jesus is absolutely true.* He's the Son of God. He's the Savior of the world. And he's willing to save me. So I told God, "I want what my sister has. I want you in my life." And that's when things started changing for me too. I started seeing the world in a different way. I noticed my desires were slowly changing.

As those sample testimonies show, in your last few sentences, you just want to mention some specific ways your life has changed since you put your faith in Jesus. If you've been a Christian your whole life, focus on specific turning points, moments when your faith made a difference in your life or behavior. Remember: Your story is your story. It will be different from everyone else's. Don't parrot the words of others and don't feel pressured to make your experience sound more dramatic than it really is.

Remember another thing: Some new believers experience instant and radical changes in their lives: They "feel" the overwhelming presence of God in their lives. Or they suddenly have no desire for alcohol. Or they immediately walk away from a toxic relationship. The change is stark and quick.

> Growth in the Christian life isn't a competition, because we're each in a category all by ourselves.

Others, however, don't necessarily "feel" much of anything. They experience subtle and slow changes in attitudes and habits. And people who grew up Christian might not even know what their life would have looked like "before." Such different experiences are a reminder that God's transformation process is unique. Just like snowflakes and fingerprints are one of a kind, no two believers undergo the same changes in the same way and on the same schedule. Growth in the Christian life isn't a competition, because we're each in a category all by ourselves. Therefore, sharing your testimony isn't about trying to tell the most eye-opening story. Rather, it's an exercise in telling the truth about your changed (and changing) life.

You might write something like:

> Since believing in Jesus, I've noticed that I don't worry as much as I did before. Now when I bump into a situation that used to make me fret and freak and toss and turn, I remember that Bible verse that says, "Don't worry about anything, instead pray about everything. Tell God what you need" (Philippians 4:6 NLT). I'm finding that when I do that—when I give my worries to God—I'm almost always calmer. Also, I seem to be less of a control freak. Before, I was always trying to get people to be a certain way and situations to turn out how I planned. I still sometimes fall back into that, but I'm learning to let go. To let God be God. To let him run the universe. When I do that, my stress levels are much lower.

What about Hell?

Many Christians are uncertain about whether to discuss hell in the context of evangelism: Is it helpful? Or is it engaging in scare tactics?

Two things are true:

1. The New Testament speaks frankly about the terrible fate that awaits those who reject God's grace (Matthew 13:49–50; 25:46; 2 Thessalonians 1:8–9).

2. An excessive focus on eternal punishment can cause people to miss the "good news" in the good news! It can produce "believers" with a defective understanding of

salvation. Instead of people being overwhelmed by God's grace and filled with a deep love for the Savior (Luke 7:36–39), you can end up with people who are primarily scared of God's wrath and motivated by fear. They don't see God's offer of eternal life as an astonishing opportunity to know Jesus (John 17:3). They see it mostly as a way to avoid pain and suffering. Such a relationship with God—built largely on the fear of eternal punishment—will never be healthy or attractive like a relationship with Jesus rooted in gratitude and love.

God-honoring evangelism will always spell out the grim stakes of unbelief. But it will go to even greater lengths to explain the glorious blessings of faith in Christ.

10 Things NOT to Do When Sharing Your Faith

1 Don't assume.

Your neighbor who seems devout and goes to church weekly may not actually understand the gospel. Your wild, rebellious coworker who seems a million miles from God might be on the verge of turning to Jesus! We never know the truth about others' hearts . . . or how God is working.

2 Don't be preachy.

It's easy, when we feel passionate about something, to get wound up. We start talking louder . . . and faster

. . . and soon we're in full-fledged sermon mode. In front of a big crowd of 100 or 1000, this kind of passion is effective, but when we're sitting in a coffee shop or at someone's kitchen counter, it's over-the-top. Far better to have good gospel conversations with people than to go around preaching at people. Engage in dialogues, not diatribes.

Avoid churchy, "insider" jargon.

Good Bible words like "sanctified" and "atonement," and phrases like "washed in the blood of the lamb" have special meaning to believers. To unbelievers, they're like a foreign language. When we talk in Christian lingo, "outsiders" feel dumb. They shut down or tune out. Be sensitive and put the gospel in terms people can grasp.

Don't dump the truck.

We have a tendency to think that if some truth is good, more is better. But when we embrace that kind of thinking while sharing our faith, we inundate people with way too much information: an avalanche of Bible verses, a tidal wave of theological insights (and mini-sermons to explain all those verses and insights). Resist this temptation! It's always better at the end of a spiritual discussion to have a person say, "Can we talk some more?" rather than leave thinking, *That was overwhelming—I thought it would never end*.

Don't get caught up in side issues.

When we each stand before God the ultimate question is going to be, "What did you do with Jesus?" not "What did you think about angels or all the different denominations or infant baptism?" Keep bringing the conversation back around to Jesus. His question to his disciples is the question that matters most: "Who do you say I am?" (Mark 8:29).

Don't be shortsighted.

A person doesn't have to "pray the sinner's prayer" for your conversation to be a success. (Remember our scale?) Researchers say that people have to hear the gospel multiple times (some say eight, others say twelve—or more) before they are ready to respond. You are helping them make progress in their spiritual journey. You are sowing seeds of truth. Just because you don't see a harvest right away doesn't mean your efforts were a waste.

Don't argue.

We can't say this enough: If you get in spiritual quarrels with people, and you "win" by showing them how "dumb" their arguments are, what have you won, really? You may have only pushed them further away from Christ and made it harder for the next Christian to have a constructive conversation with them! If it's clear someone just wants to spar, spiritually speaking, walk away. Nobody ever got argued into the kingdom of God.

Don't take rejection personally.

If you have a spiritual conversation with someone and they get huffy or clam up or start avoiding you, ask yourself one question: Was I rude or insensitive or pushy when I talked about my faith? If the answer is "maybe a little" or "no doubt—I came on way too strong," it's not the end of the world. Just apologize. A simple "I'm sorry about the other day. I know I tend to get excited when I talk about my faith. I don't want be pushy like that. Please forgive me" will suffice. But if the answer is "not at all," then your friend's reaction likely says more about them than about you. Perhaps the coldness or rejection you feel from them is really conviction in disguise. Maybe God is working in deep ways. Keep being a friend and keep praying.

> "And the Lord's servant must not be quarrelsome but must be kind to everyone, able to teach, not resentful. Opponents must be gently instructed, in the hope that God will grant them repentance leading them to a knowledge of the truth, and that they will come to their senses and escape from the trap of the devil, who has taken them captive to do his will."
>
> 2 TIMOTHY 2:24–26

Think invitation, not condemnation.

When followers of Jesus approach their neighbors or coworkers with an attitude of "Here are the eleven ways your life is screwed up," nonbelievers naturally get defensive. (Wouldn't you?) Instead of denouncing the life an unbeliever's living, entice them with the new life Jesus offers.

Don't forget your role.

In the great cosmic drama of which we're a part, God hasn't assigned us the part of Savior or Healer or Holy Spirit. Our role is to love and to listen, to show the gospel and to share it. It's up to God to stir people's hearts and get them to the point where they want to trust in Jesus. Only he can change a life. The better we remember this great truth, the easier sharing our faith becomes.

What Is *Apologetics*?

Maybe you've heard other Christians talk about using apologetics in sharing their faith. This doesn't mean apologizing for what we believe. (Though—to tell the truth—when we're talking to people who have deep church wounds, it's always good to say, "I'm so sorry you had that experience.")

Apologetics is the practice of explaining and defending what one believes in a rational and logical way. The word comes from the Greek, and we see it used in the New Testament in 1 Peter 3:15, where the apostle Peter tells believers to be ready to "explain" (NLT) or "give a defense" (NKJV) or "give an account" (NASB) or "give the reason" (NIV) or "give an answer" (NET) for the hope they have.

Explaining, defending, answering—apologetics is all that. It's not "proving" that God exists or that Jesus was God in the flesh. We can't prove such things, but we can make a strong case for Christianity, showing why it's reasonable or why—as apologist Josh McDowell used to say—we don't have to put our brains on a shelf to become a Christian. Good apologists graciously answer hard questions about the Christian faith. They skillfully argue (without being argumentative) for the trustworthiness of the Bible and the truthfulness of the gospel.

Common questions asked by cynics, seekers, and skeptics are:

- Can we be sure that God exists?

- If God exists and is all-powerful and good—as Christians claim—why is there so much evil and suffering in the world?

- Aren't all religions saying basically the same thing in different words? Aren't they all just different ways to God?

- Are miracles really possible?

- Why should anyone trust the Bible?

- Who was Jesus? Why so much focus on his life and death? Did he really rise from the dead?

- How can Christians insist that Jesus is the only way to God?

For some people these big, troubling questions are a genuine barrier to placing faith in Christ. These "seekers" need help processing these enigmas and mysteries. They need an *apologist*—someone who can sit down with them, listen to their concerns, and give valid reasons and reasonable explanations (not absolute proof).

For others, however, questions like these serve only as a smokescreen or defense mechanism—a way of avoiding the claims of Jesus—by trying to divert attention elsewhere. Josh McDowell used to tell the story of encountering and debating a very smart, extremely argumentative skeptic. The young college student kept firing questions at Josh until Josh finally said, "Tell me something: If I were to give you reasonable answers to all of your questions, would you give your life to Christ?" The student thought for a moment, shook his head, and said, "No, I wouldn't." Josh nodded and replied, "Just as I thought. You don't have an intellectual problem with Christianity, you have a problem of the will."

It is a waste of precious time—and breath—to engage in verbal battles with hardhearted skeptics who aren't really open to an honest examination of the claims of Christ. At some point we have to realize: They're not listening, so I don't need to keep talking.

Again, nobody was ever argued into the kingdom of God.

If you'd like to be better equipped at answering the tough questions of skeptics, six great resources are:

- *Mere Christianity* by C. S. Lewis

- *Evidence That Demands a Verdict* by Josh McDowell

- *Is Believing in God Irrational?* by Amy Orr-Ewing

- *The Reason for God* by Timothy Killer

- *Reasonable Faith* by William Lane Craig

- *Christian Apologetics* by Norman Geisler

- *The Case for Christ* and *The Case for Faith* by Lee Strobel

And even if you end up reading 100 books on apologetics, never be afraid (or ashamed) to say, "That's a great question, and honestly . . . I don't know the answer. But if that's what's keeping you from putting your faith in Jesus, I'll be glad to look for an answer and get back to you."

10 Reminders

1 Pray.

You've no doubt heard that old saying, "Talk to God about people before you talk to people about God." (If not, you have now!) Make a list of folks who don't (yet) know Jesus. Use the lists found earlier in this book to pray for them . . . and for yourself.

2 Live the gospel.

Serve others like Jesus did. Author Joe Aldrich used to say, "Love people till they ask you why." What wisdom! The more you show the gospel with your life, the more you'll get chances to share the gospel with your mouth. People will wonder (and eventually ask), "What makes you tick?"

3 Cultivate relationships with people who don't know Jesus.

It's kind of hard to have conversations with unbelievers if you never see any, or if you only hang around fellow believers. Get out there. Mix and mingle. Join a civic club, a book club, or the Garden Society. Join a city sports league. Be intentional.

4 Listen!

"My dear brothers and sisters, take note of this: Everyone should be quick to listen, slow to speak and slow to become angry, because human anger does not produce the righteousness that God desires" (James 1:19–20).

Don't overcomplicate matters.

Remember, sharing your faith is, in its purest essence, passing on good news. When we hear: "All your biopsies were clear" or "You're going to be a grandparent!"—nobody has to tap us on the shoulder and whisper, "Um, you might want to tell a few people about that." We instinctively do it, right? Good news is for sharing—in fact, it's harder to not share it! Have you ever heard of a seminar entitled "How to Tell Others Your Cancer Is in Remission"? Of course not.

Talk about Jesus.

You've got to love the way Luke describes Philip's conversation with the Ethiopian official in Acts 8:35. Lectures about morality? No. Debates over earth's origins? No way. Philip "told him the good news about Jesus." Stay on topic!

Paint an honest picture of the future.

Don't soft-pedal the truth that when Jesus comes into a life, he starts changing everything (see Luke 14). He will meddle in our relationships, our sex lives, how we do business, and how we handle money. Those who believe in him belong to him.

Be people smart.

Learn to read people. If you see folded arms, eyes that are flashing or rolling . . . it you notice a tight jaw, a red face, or a voice that is shaking and getting louder by the minute, catch a clue: Your conversation isn't going anywhere good. Change the subject. It's not a good time.

Be careful online.

A lot of angry trolls live out there in cyberspace. They make it easy to forget about winning souls and to focus instead on winning religious arguments. Don't take the bait. When you can't see the person you're engaging with, it's too easy to became snarky, dismissive, and harsh. If you can't respond in love, put down your smartphone. Nobody ever got insulted into the kingdom of God. And God doesn't need you to "defend" him.

Keep at it.

Like anything, talking about your faith becomes more natural the more you do it.

The Greatest Treasure

In Matthew 13:44–46, Jesus told two short parables (simple stories with deep meaning) about why his coming and his gospel should thrill our hearts. Paraphrased, Jesus said something like this:

"You want to know what the kingdom of heaven is like? What it looks like when people recognize and embrace who I am?

"Picture a guy accidentally finding buried treasure on a piece of land just outside the city limits. Suddenly the old guy is doing cartwheels in his head, texting his neighbor who's in real estate, and arranging a hasty, 'everything must go' estate sale so he can scrape together the money needed to purchase the property."

"Or imagine a jeweler who appraises, buys, and sells precious gems all day every day. One day a stranger comes by with a pearl so exquisite, so precious, it briefly stops the jeweler's heart. He feels so woozy, he has to go run cold water on his face. When he returns from the restroom, mind racing, heart pounding in his chest, the jeweler tells the stranger, 'Tell you what . . . give me that pearl and you can have my entire shop, all my inventory, everything.'"

Neither man pauses to think, "Look at what I'm giving up!" Their one consuming thought is, "Look at all I could have!"

The gospel is a message about the greatest treasure in the world: Jesus. Next time you feel less than amazed about the gospel and unmotivated to tell others, consider again the great worth of Jesus.

He's a friend of sinners (Matthew 11:19). Many people—including some in your life—assume that God despises sinful people. Not true. Jesus went out of his way to be with irreligious people, and rather than avoid him, they flocked to him.

He's an all-powerful savior (Luke 19:10). Everyone around you needs to be rescued from something—shame, guilt, fear, addiction, anger, unhealthy habits, toxic relationships, a life void of meaning (we could go on and on). Guess what? Jesus came to save. He can deliver your family members and coworkers from anything. He sets captives free (Luke 4:18).

He's a great physician (Luke 5:31). During his brief ministry on earth, Jesus healed those who were sick physically, emotionally, and spiritually. His question to the world is still, "Do you want to get well?" (John 5:6). (Maybe his question to us is, "Do you want your friends and neighbors to get well?")

He's a good shepherd (John 10:11, 14). Most people don't have a clue what they're doing or where they're going. They're vulnerable, just bumbling along, following the crowd, and headed for danger. They need to know Jesus, the One who will protect them from predators and guide them to good places.

He's the king (Revelation 19:16). The angel who announced the birth of Jesus introduced him as "a Savior . . . the Messiah, the Lord" (Luke 2:11). That's a mouthful right there—but it basically means Jesus is the one sent from God to rescue, restore, and rule *everything*.

He's the ultimate reflection of who God is (John 1:1, 14). The New Testament makes the extraordinary claim that if we want to know what God is like, we need only look at Jesus (John 14:9; Colossians 1:15; Hebrews 1:3).

Finally, here's the most comforting news of all about sharing our faith . . .

The Pressure's Off!

You can't save anyone. Only God can do that. Jesus said that people can't come to him until the Father in heaven draws them (John 6:44). And people will never trust in Jesus until the Holy Spirit convicts them of their sin—and shows them their desperate need to be right with God (John 16:8).

Those truths are good news for us. It means the pressure's off. We don't have to argue with people or get preachy and screechy. We don't have to resort to spiritual threats or manipulative techniques. Saving souls is God's business.

Our part is simply to move toward unbelievers. We engage, befriend, love, ask good questions, listen attentively, tell the truth, share our experience, and pray like crazy. (The great missionary to China, Hudson Taylor, used to tell his coworkers, "You must go forward on your knees.")

One of the most freeing truths you will ever hear is something Bill Bright, the founder of Campus Crusade for Christ (or Cru), used to say: "Success in witnessing is simply taking the initiative to share Christ in the power of the Holy Spirit, and leaving the results to God."

God is in charge of outcomes. We're called simply to be faithful and do our part. And our part is as easy as:

1. Praying for others

2. Talking to others

3. Entrusting others to God

GOSPEL ILLUSTRATIONS

Some concepts and ideas in the Bible are difficult to express in words. Things like love, forgiveness, and sin are very abstract and complex. Metaphors make abstract concepts easier to understand. By using common experiences— such as gardening, becoming ill, joining a family, becoming a citizen, or having debt—metaphors allow people to connect with the concepts at a personal level. It is important to explore, learn, appropriate, and use the illustrations the Bible itself uses to explain what Jesus accomplished on the cross.

What does "salvation" mean? How does the Bible explain it? How do we explain it to others? The following pages list illustrations of salvation in the Bible.

A *metaphor* is a figure of speech in which a word or phrase, literally denoting one kind of object or idea, is used in place of another to suggest a likeness or analogy between them.

An *illustration* is an example or instance that helps explain and make something clear.

Biology

Metaphor	**BIOLOGY**	Jesus promises us a new and abundant life (John 10:10).
Positive	**LIFE**	• Abundant life (John 5:24–26) • Bread of life (John 6:35) • God wants us to be fruitful (John 15:8; Col. 1:10).
Negative	**DEATH**	• Deserving death (Rom. 1:32) • Death through Adam (Rom. 5:12–14) • Sin causes lack of fruit (Gen. 3:16–19; Luke 3:9; John 15:2).
Illustrations		• Death is a human reality. But Jesus offers life, eternal life. • As a metaphor, death represents the end of all possibilities and hope. People live as if they were dead, without hope and separated from God. • Jesus offers abundant life. Jesus offers a new opportunity to live life like God intended it from the beginning. • Jesus raised Lazarus from the dead (John 11). Besides being a miracle, it also illustrates what Jesus does for people: He gives new life. • As we receive new life, God wants us to be fruitful and share this new life with the people around us.

Human Development

Metaphor	**HUMAN DEVELOPMENT**	Jesus promises to complete the transforming work of maturity in each believer (Phil. 1:6).
Positive	**MATURITY**	• Parable of the Sower (Luke 8:14) • Becoming mature (Eph. 4:13) • Perseverance to maturity (James 1:4) • No longer foolish (Titus 3:3)
Negative	**IMMATURITY**	• Idols made by humans are foolishness (Jer. 10:8). • In need of teaching (Rom. 2:20–22) • Ignorance of God's will (Eph. 5:17)
Illustrations		• One of the effects of sin is that it stunts growth. God intended humans to live a full life. Sin does not allow us to reach our true potential. It makes people act like fools, in immature ways. • Sin has stunted our growth. Although we claim wisdom, our sin has made us fools (Rom. 1:22). • When Jesus cares for us, we become like trees planted by abundant waters that have the maturity to stand during droughts (Ps. 1:3).

Health

Metaphor	**HEALTH**	Jesus promises to be our physician and heal our minds, hearts, and souls (Mark 2:17).
Positive	**HEALING**	• Through Jesus' sacrifice, we are healed from our sins (Isa. 53:5; 1 Peter 2:24). • Prayer and confession to be healed (James 5:16) • God forgives our sins and heals our illness (Ps. 103:3).
Negative	**ILLNESS**	• Sickness (Matt. 9:2, 5; 1 Peter 2:24)
Illustrations		• The common experience of illness offers many possibilities to illustrate Christ's work. • "It is not the healthy who need a doctor but the sick . . ." Jesus used these words to describe his own ministry. The prophet Isaiah had promised: "No one living in Zion will say, 'I am ill'; and the sins of those who dwell there will be forgiven" (Isa. 33:24). • There are illnesses that our body can fight off alone. There are others, however, that require help. There are personality faults and character issues that one can deal with. There is a deep, moral problem, called sin, that only one physician can cure: Jesus.

Family

Metaphor	**FAMILY**	Through Jesus, believers become children of God and can call him, "Abba, Father" (Gal. 4:6).
Positive	**ADOPTION**	• Christians become part of God's family (Rom. 8:15; Eph. 1:5). • Have the full rights of a son (Gal. 4:5) • Receive the assurance that God will resurrect believers' bodies (Rom. 8:11)
Negative	**ORPHAN**	• The orphan, along with the widow and the poor, are the most vulnerable and needy in society (Deut. 10:18; James 1:26–27). • Life apart from God is like that of an orphan: full of uncertainty, danger, and lack of love (Hos. 14:1–3).
Illustrations		• Orphans are some of the most neglected, unprotected, and unloved people in societies throughout history. • Family connections were necessary for survival and a chance to succeed. • Christians call God "Father" because God has adopted us into his family. • The word *Abba* is a close affectionate term like *daddy*. • Now, regardless of who our family is, whether they are good or not, we all have one, good Father.

Relationship

Metaphor	**RELATIONSHIP**	Jesus promises to be more than our master. He promises to be our friend (John 15:15).
Positive	**FRIEND**	• Jesus gave his life for his friends (John 15:13). • We show our friendship through our obedience (John 15:14).
Negative	**ENEMY**	• We were God's enemies (Rom. 5:10; Col. 1:21); in Jesus, we are reconciled with God. • Jesus will defeat his enemies (1 Cor. 15:25).

Illustrations

- Sin has created a gap between God and humans.
- This gap is enmity between God and us.
- Jesus became a bridge that allows us to walk over to God.
- Then, we can have a relationship with God as his friends.

Rescue

Metaphor	**RESCUE**	Jesus promises to rescue us and keep us safe forever (Deut. 31:6; Heb. 13:5).
Positive	**SAVED**	• Jesus came to save the world (John 3:17). • Saves us from our sins (Eph. 2:1–9) • Saves us from God's just wrath (Rom. 5:9) • Saves us from death (Heb. 2:14–15) • Whoever believes in Jesus will not perish (John 3:16). • Jesus gives eternal life (John 10:28).
Negative	**PERISHING**	• God does not want anyone to perish (2 Peter 3:9). • Eternal Death (Matt. 7:13; 25:41, 46; Rev. 20:14–15) • Gehenna (Garbage Dump) (Matt. 5:22, 29, 30; 10:28; 18:9; 23:15, 33; Mark 9:43–47; Luke 12:5)
Illustrations		• Jesus speaks of the wicked perishing in "Gehenna." • Gehenna is another word for hell, but it was also the garbage dump of the city of Jerusalem, where garbage was continually burning. • Our sin had broken us and made us useless to God. • We were ready for the garbage dump. • Jesus came to rescue us from the never-ending trash pile. • Jesus' cross stands as a bridge that leads us to eternal safety.

Freedom

Metaphor	**FREEDOM**	Jesus has promised to make us free from all bondage (John 8:36).
Positive	**DELIVERANCE**	To free us to: • New life (Rom. 6:4) • Freedom to serve (Gal. 5:1, 13) • Eternal life (John 10:28)
Negative	**SLAVERY**	To free us from: • Sin (Rom. 6:18) • The curse of the law (Gal. 4:3–5) • The fear of death (Heb. 2:14–15)
Illustrations		• Many things bind us: self-interest, addictions, broken relationships, anger and bitterness, destructive pasts, and debts. Sin captures our minds and hearts. Only a miracle can break those bonds. • Jesus breaks these bonds and gives us new life. This new life gives us the freedom to serve God, to become the people God wants us to be.

Economy

Metaphor	**ECONOMY**	Jesus bought each believer at a price; the sale is final (1 Cor. 6:20; 7:23).
Positive	**PAYMENT**	• Offered himself as ransom (payment) on our behalf (Matt. 20:28; Heb. 9:15) • His sacrifice on the cross paid in full the debt that sin caused.
Negative	**DEBT**	• Sin caused a "debt" with God—Jesus cancels this debt (Col. 2:14). • The price for redemption is high (1 Peter 1:19).
Illustrations		• Difficult economic times make the burden of debts a very concrete reality. Although we often ignore it, the burden of sin is much heavier. • Getting rid of the huge weight of financial debt would allow people to start over, be wiser, and live better. Similarly, when Jesus lifts the weight of sin from us through his death, we are free to live life to the fullest. Jesus offers the opportunity to live without the burden of sin so we can live the abundant life that Jesus promises.

Law

Metaphor	**LAW**	In Jesus we find complete forgiveness so God "will tread our sins underfoot and hurl our iniquities into the depths of the sea" (Micah 7:19).
Positive	**FORGIVENESS**	• Sins are forgiven forever (Jer. 31:34; Heb. 8:12). • Forgiveness comes from God's grace (Eph. 1:7). • God desires for everyone to be forgiven (1 Tim. 2:4).
Negative	**CRIME AND PUNISHMENT**	• A compassionate but just God (Num. 14:18) • God punishes sin (Lam. 3:39). • God is the ultimate judge (Prov. 24:12; Rom. 14:12).
Illustrations		• Most people have had to deal with a legal issue—a parking ticket, the selling of a home, or other more serious cases. • While not pleasant, we understand that the legal requirements and process are necessary and healthy. • The Bible uses this metaphor to show both the necessity and the rightness of Jesus' ministry of forgiveness and eventual judgment. • The legal consequences of sin are so big and eternal that we cannot deal with them on our own. Jesus is the only person who can and has done something about them. • Jesus' death on the cross has made it possible for us to receive God's forgiveness. • The Bible presents Jesus' work as an advocate on our behalf. He is our "defense lawyer" (Heb. 7:25; 1 John 2:1).

Military

Metaphor	**MILITARY**	Jesus has promised to give us lasting peace (John 14:27).
Positive	**PEACE**	• Peace with God through faith in Jesus (Rom. 5:1) • Jesus destroyed barriers of hostility (Eph. 2:14–22). • Jesus has defeated the powers of this world (1 Cor. 15:24–28). • Believers are also victorious (Rom. 8:31–39).
Negative	**WAR**	• We were God's enemies (Rom. 5:10; Col. 1:21). • We were under the dominion of darkness (Col. 1:12–14). • We were followers of the devil and his ways (Eph. 2:1–7).
Illustrations		• Life often feels like a battle: a battle with our own struggles and sin (Rom. 7:21–25), with external influences and pressures. • Yet, Jesus' victory on the cross has defeated all the powers that bind and limit humanity: sin and death are defeated; Satan and his hosts are defeated. • Jesus' death on the cross was D-Day for God's people. In the famous day in World War II, the Allies overtook the beaches of Normandy and changed the course of the war. Jesus mortally wounded Satan and sealed his fate.

Nationality

Metaphor	**NATIONALITY**	Jesus allows us to become citizens of the kingdom of heaven.
Positive	**CITIZEN**	• Fellow citizens (Eph. 2:19) • Citizens of heaven (Phil. 3:20)
Negative	**ALIEN**	• Alien to a sinful world (1 Peter 2:11) • People looking for a country of their own (Heb. 11:13) • Longing for our real home (2 Peter 3:13)
Illustrations		• Being a citizen of a country provides identity, security, and rootedness. • Christians are citizens of God's kingdom. Our loyalties are to God and his will. • In a globalized world, where people move so fast and everywhere, the concept of citizenship takes new meanings. • Our identity, security, and sense of community do not depend on the place or culture in which we were born. Rather, it depends on the values of the kingdom of God.

Vision

Metaphor	**VISION**	Jesus promises to open our eyes so we can see him and God's wonders (Isa. 42:7).
Positive	**SIGHT**	• Jesus opened the eyes of his disciples (Luke 24:31). • Jesus came to give sight (Luke 4:18–19; John 9:39).
Negative	**BLINDNESS**	• Sin is blindness (John 9:39–41). • Blind guides lead others astray (Matt. 23:16–17). • People blinded to the gospel (2 Cor. 4:4).
Illustrations		• In the Bible, physical blindness was a metaphor for spiritual blindness. • Jesus used this metaphor to teach about the gospel (see John 9). • In the ancient world, only the "gods" were able to heal blindness. • Jesus restores both physical and spiritual sight to people. • Spiritual blindness has different causes: fear, unbelief, pride, greed, hatred, and egocentrism. Spiritual blindness prevents us from seeing God's doings in the world.

Knowledge

Metaphor	**KNOWLEDGE**	Jesus gives us the knowledge of God to be saved, to grow and mature, and live a life that pleases God (1 Tim. 2:4; 2 Tim. 2:25).
Positive	**UNDERSTANDING**	• Jesus gives the knowledge of salvation (Luke 1:77). • The Spirit gives understanding of what Christ has done (1 Cor. 2:12). • We have wisdom from God (Eph. 1:8, 17; Col. 2:2–3; James 1:5).
Negative	**IGNORANCE**	• Lack of knowledge causes destruction (Hos. 4:6). • Life apart from God is a life of ignorance (1 Peter 1:14). • Foolishness separates us from God (Jer. 5:21; 10:8; Titus 3:3).
Illustrations		• The knowledge that the Bible refers to here is not only mental knowledge. It also means intimate knowledge. It is a knowledge that affects the mind and the heart. • To truly get to know a person, reading a biography, hearing from other people, or spending a few minutes with a person is not enough. One needs time and energy to develop a relationship. After that time, one *knows* the other person. • It is not only book knowledge that allows us to know God and obtain salvation; we need deep, relational knowledge of Jesus. • The Holy Spirit gives us this knowledge primarily through the Scriptures, prayer, and fellowship with other believers.

Truth

Metaphor	**TRUTH**	Jesus offers the only truth that can lead us to God (John 14:6).
Positive	**CORRECT/ TRUE**	• Salvation as knowledge of the truth (1 Tim. 2:4) • The gospel is the word of truth (Eph. 1:13; John 17:17). • The truth of the gospel makes us free (John 8:32). • The Holy Spirit leads us to the truth (John 16:13).
Negative	**ERROR/FALSE**	• False prophets deceive and lead astray (Ezek. 13:1–23; Matt. 24:11, 24). • False teachings lead to destruction (2 Peter 2:1–2).
Illustrations		• Traveling without a map can lead to an exciting adventure or a disastrous end. A map is helpful when we follow its instructions. A correct map will lead us faithfully. An incorrect map will lead us astray. • The words of the gospel lead us correctly to our final destination.

Navigation

Metaphor	**NAVIGATION**	Jesus came to seek and save the lost. He promises to guide us to the right destination (Luke 19:10).
Positive	**FOUND**	• The lost have been returned (1 Peter 2:25). • The Good Shepherd seeks the lost sheep (Matt. 18:12). • Jesus came to save what was lost (Luke 19:10). • Joy in heaven for the found (Luke 15:1–7) • Joy over the lost who is found (Luke 15:11–32)
Negative	**LOST**	• We were lost (Isa. 53:6; Jer. 50:6; Mark 6:34).
Illustrations		• The sense of being lost, especially in a hostile environment, produces many strong emotions: fear, anxiety, anger, and disappointment. • The final problem is that lost people are incapable of reaching their destination. • Jesus reorients us toward our correct destination: God's kingdom. When Jesus saves us, we begin to walk in the direction that will lead us to our final destination in God's presence.

Walking

Metaphor	**WALKING**	Jesus promises to walk alongside us: "And surely I am with you always, to the very end of the age" (Matt. 28:20).
Positive	**STANDING/ WALKING**	• Walking on the path of righteousness (Prov. 8:20; 12:28) • The path of life revealed (Acts 2:28; Ps. 16:11) • Jesus keeps us from falling (Jude 1:24).
Negative	**FALLING/ STUMBLING**	• Those burdened by sin stagger and fall (Isa. 3:8). • Those who do not know Christ will stumble over him (Rom. 9:32, 33; Isa. 8:14). • Unbelief in Jesus causes us to fall (1 Peter 2:8; Luke 20:18).
Illustrations		• Walking in God's paths is a common metaphor in the Bible. • *Walking* brings to mind the idea of movement and journeying, the satisfactions and benefits of traveling as well as the difficulties involved in it. • As we walk, we learn, grow, and move forward. • However, walking requires a direction, lest it becomes mere wandering. • One way to understand sin is that one misses the mark, or one's destination. • Jesus gives us a new orientation. • The Holy Spirit is our compass, and the Scriptures are our map. • Only by walking alongside Jesus can we reach God, our true destination.

Light

Metaphor	**LIGHT**	Jesus is the light that shines on our path toward God (John 12:46).
Positive	**LIGHT**	• Jesus is the light of the world (John 8:12). • Jesus' light shines in our hearts (2 Cor. 4:4–6). • Children of light (Eph. 5:8) • Jesus has rescued us from darkness (Col. 1:13). • Putting aside the deeds of darkness (Rom. 13:12)
Negative	**DARK**	• People living in darkness have seen a great light (Matt. 4:16). • Humans have loved darkness (John 3:19).
Illustrations		• A campfire in the wilderness provides light, warmth, safety, and sustenance. • The light helps campers to find their way back to the camp. It provides warmth for the night. It keeps wild animals away. It cooks food and purifies water. • In a similar way, Jesus provides us with guiding light, warmth, safety, and sustenance for our journey of life.

Purity

Metaphor	**PURITY**	Jesus promises to cleanse us completely from our sins (Heb. 9:14).
Positive	**PURE/CLEAN**	• Jesus purifies his people (Titus 2:14). • Jesus' blood purifies us from sin (1 John 1:9).
Negative	**IMPURITY/ DIRTY**	• Jesus did not call us to be impure (1 Thess. 4:7). • We were slaves to impurity (Rom. 6:19).
Illustrations		• Cleanliness and dirtiness are daily experiences in life. The idea of cleaning something to make it acceptable is easy to visualize. • We clean our homes, our clothing, and our bodies to make them presentable and pleasant for others. • Sin corrupts and makes people impure. • People cannot make themselves clean of this pollution on their own. • However, God cleans us with Jesus' blood to make us acceptable, pleasant to himself.

Agriculture

Metaphor	**AGRICULTURE**	By being connected to Jesus, God's people have new life, can be fruitful, and have an abundant life.
Positive	**CONNECTION**	• God is portrayed as a caring gardener (Isa. 5:1–7). • Jesus allows us to be saved by grafting us into the tree to become part of his people (Rom. 11:24). • God's people are like trees planted by streams of water (Ps. 1:3). • Only by being connected to Jesus, the true vine, can we bear fruit (John 15:1–8).
Negative	**SEPARATION**	• By pruning Israel, God allowed Gentiles to become part of God's people (Rom. 11:17–21). • People without Jesus are like chaff that the wind blows away (Ps. 1:4). • No one can bear fruit apart from Jesus (John 15:4–6).
Illustrations		• Grafting and pruning are common activities in gardening. • Gardeners, professional and amateur, understand how important pruning is for the care and productivity of plants. • Like a gardener caring for his plants, God cares for his people. • God takes each of us, lifeless chaff, and grafts us into the tree of his people to give us new life. • Being saved is like being a plant, which is cared for and fruitful, in God's garden.

Creation

Metaphor	**CREATION**	Jesus gives us the opportunity to be born again, to be a new creation. It is more than a fresh start. It is the right start (John 3:16–18).
Positive	**NEW CREATION**	• Jesus used the language of being born again (John 3:3, 7; 1 Peter 1:23). • Those born of God are children of God (1 John 3:9–10). • Christians are a new creation (2 Cor. 5:17; Gal. 6:15). • Jesus is presented as the second Adam (Rom. 5:15–17). • Jesus is the firstborn of the new creation (1 Cor. 15:27; 2 Cor. 5:17; Col. 1:15; Phil. 3:21).
Negative	**OLD CREATION**	• Sin transformed all of creation (Gen. 3:18; Rom. 8:22). • Sin entered through Adam's disobedience (Rom. 5:12–14). • This creation will pass and God will make all things new (Rev. 21:1; 2 Peter 3:13). • Nothing of the old creation can enter the kingdom of God (John 3:5).
Illustrations		• Jesus illustrated this point with a common object of his time: an unshrunk cloth to patch an old garment (Matt. 9:16). • The illustration is clear: when the garment is washed, the patch will shrink and tear the garment beyond repair. The old and the new do not mix with each other. • Just as God makes us a new creation, God will make all things new one day (Rev. 21:1).

Evangelism Plans

These evangelism plans are ways to illustrate the gospel so its message is easier to understand. They have helped millions of Christians around the world to bring the message of the gospel in a simple yet effective way.

FOUR SPIRITUAL LAWS
(Campus Crusade for Christ)

1 **God loves you and offers a wonderful plan for your life** (John 3:16; 10:10).

2 **Humans are sinful and separated from God.** Thus, they cannot know and experience God's love and plan for their lives (Rom. 3:23; 6:23).

3 **Jesus Christ is God's only provision for humanity's sin.** Through Jesus, you can know and experience God's love and plan for your life (Rom. 5:8; John 14:6).

4 **We must individually receive Jesus Christ as Savior and Lord.** Then we can know and experience God's love and plan for our lives (John 1:12; Eph. 2:8–9).

BRIDGE TO LIFE (Navigators)

The Bible teaches that God loves all humans and wants them to know him (John 10:10; Rom. 5:1).

But humans have sinned against God and are separated from God and his love. This separation leads only to death and judgment (Rom. 3:23; Isa. 59:2).

But there is a solution: Jesus Christ died on the cross for our sins (the bridge between humanity and God) (1 Peter 3:18; 1 Tim. 2:5; Rom. 5:8).

Only those who personally receive Jesus Christ into their lives, trusting him to forgive their sins, can cross this bridge. Everyone must decide individually whether to receive Christ (John 3:16; 5:24).

Jesus' work on the cross allows sinful people to begin a relationship with God and be rescued from eternal death.

STEPS TO PEACE WITH GOD
(Billy Graham Crusade)

STEP 1
God's Plan: Peace and Life
(Rom. 5:1; John 3:16; 10:10)

STEP 2
Humanity's Problem: Separation
(Rom. 3:23; 6:23; Isa. 59:2)

STEP 3
God's Remedy: The Cross
(1 Tim. 2:5; 1 Peter 3:18; Rom. 5:8)

STEP 4
Human Response: Receive Christ
(John 1:12; 5:24; Rom. 10:9)

THE ROMANS ROAD OF SALVATION

Human Need: "For all have sinned and fall short of the glory of God" (Rom. 3:23).

Sin's Penalty: "For the wages of sin is death, but the gift of God is eternal life in Christ Jesus our Lord" (Rom. 6:23).

God's Provision: "But God demonstrates his own love for us in this: While we were still sinners, Christ died for us" (Rom. 5:8).

The Person's Response: "If you declare with your mouth, 'Jesus is Lord,' and believe in your heart that God raised him from the dead, you will be saved" (Rom. 10:9).

FOUR CIRCLES

James Choung's Four Circles illustration shows God's original intention for his creation. God made humans to be and do good. However, sin affected our ability to do good. We became self-centered and enslaved to sin. Our sin breaks our relationship with God, nature, and one another.

Jesus came to restore humanity. His death on the cross liberated us from the slavery of sin and death.

Being free from sin, believers can become ambassadors of God. God is sending believers to heal relationships by preaching the good news of Jesus to a lost humanity.

Humans cannot move from circle 2 to 4 because sin has opened a gap that separates God from humans. Only through Christ is it possible to reach God.

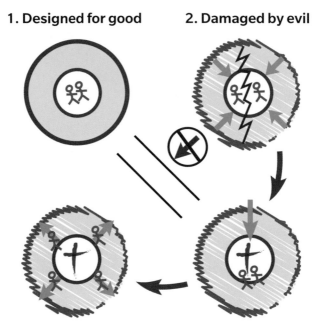

1. Designed for good
2. Damaged by evil
4. Sent together to heal
3. Restored for better

QUESTIONS FOR FURTHER REFLECTION AND DISCUSSION

1. When was the last time you got really good news? What was it and how did you go about telling others?

2. What are the top three reasons you don't talk about your faith more often?

3. Who first communicated the gospel to you—and how? If you heard about Jesus from multiple "witnesses," which ones were effective, which were not, and why?

4. Do you know any Christians who are really natural and effective at having spiritual conversations with unbelievers? What makes them so good at sharing their faith?

5. Have you ever tried to talk about your faith with someone who doesn't believe in Christ? What was that experience like?

6. Do you talk about hell when sharing the gospel? Why or why not?

7. What are the chief objections of non-Christians to the message of Jesus?

8. How is evangelism "spiritual warfare"? What are our weapons in this battle? Who is the enemy? And what is our goal?

9. In your view, what could believers in Jesus do better in their interactions with unbelievers that would result in more positive spiritual conversations?

10. How would you respond if an old friend called you out of the blue and said, "I heard you've become a Christian. Tell me about that!"?

11. What's your biggest takeaway from this book?

Image Credits